The Unmarked Grave

BE A FORENSIC ANTHROPOLOGIST

by Alix Wood

Gareth Stevens
PUBLISHING

Please visit our website, **www.garethstevens.com**. For a free color
catalog of all our high-quality books, call toll free 1-800-542-2595
or fax 1-877-542-2596

Cataloging-in-Publication Data

Names: Wood, Alix.
Title: The unmarked grave: be a forensic anthropologist / Alix Wood.
Description: New York : Gareth Stevens Publishing, 2018. | Series: Crime solvers | Includes index.
Identifiers: ISBN 9781538206409 (pbk.) | ISBN 9781538206348 (library bound) | ISBN 9781538206225 (6 pack)
Subjects: LCSH: Forensic anthropology--Juvenile literature. | Victims of crimes--Identification--Juvenile literature. |
    Criminal investigation--Juvenile literature. | Forensic sciences--Juvenile literature.
Classification: LCC GN69.8 W66 2018 | DDC 614.17--dc23

First Edition

Published in 2018 by
Gareth Stevens Publishing
111 East 14th Street, Suite 349
New York, NY 10003

Copyright © 2018 Alix Wood Books

Produced for Gareth Stevens by Alix Wood Books
Designed by Alix Wood
Editor: Eloise Macgregor
Consultant: Stacey Deville, MFS, Texas Forensic Investigative Consultants

Photo credits: Cover, 1, 4, 6, 7, 8, 9, 10, 11, 13, 15 bottom, 16, 18, 24, 25, 26, 28, 29, 35, 36, 37, 43 © Adobe Stock Images,
12, 15 top, 21, 22, 40, 41 © Alix Wood, 17 © Tom Humphries, 19 © Coronation Dental Speciality Group, 23, 39 © Shutterstock, 30 left © torange, 30 right © freestockphotos, all other images are in the public domain

Printed in the United States of America
CPSIA compliance information: Batch #CS17GS For further information contact Gareth Stevens, New York, New York at 1-800-542-2595.

CONTENTS

Call the Forensic Anthropologist...

On a sunny March afternoon, two construction workers are laying cable along the side of the highway. One worker, Steve, calls his co-worker over. He has found an obstruction, and doesn't like the look of it. They brush away some more earth, and find what looks like a human skull...

DISPATCHER: Emergency 911. What is the location of your emergency?

STEVE: I'm Steve Harrison. I'm working on the highway improvements at Saunderstone.

DISPATCHER: What is your emergency, caller?

STEVE: We think we may just have found a human skeleton.

DISPATCHER: What makes you think you have found a skeleton?

STEVE: I can see a skull staring up at me...

Reporting Officer's Notes

2:05 pm: Dispatch received a 911 call about a skeleton found near the Saunderstone highway. The caller identified himself as Steve Harrison.

Unit 574 was **dispatched** and arrived at the scene at 2:37 pm. The officers found what appeared to be a human skull. They roped off the scene and asked for backup and medical assistance.

3:05 pm: Detectives Karen Smithson and Kuan Wu arrived at the scene. The Crime Scene Investigator team was called and arrived at 3:22 pm. They examined the skull. It certainly appeared to be human. It had also clearly been in the ground a long time. They realized that they needed to call in a specialist.

3:55 pm: The forensic anthropologist, David Marek, is called. He is on his way.

Case File

Solve It!

Why might investigators rush to a crime scene if the victim had been dead a long time?

a) the victim may have been buried more recently, so there still may be important evidence nearby

b) there's no reason to rush

Answers on page 45

The detectives make sure the construction team stops working near the area. They need to protect any **evidence**. They declare the area a **crime scene**. No one may enter or leave without permission. The **medical examiner** arrives to examine the skull, and sees that the person has been dead a long time. This case needs a forensic anthropologist.

Meet a Forensic Anthropologist

A text message comes through on David Marek's cell phone. He is busy teaching a forensic anthropology class at the university where he works. He looks down at the message. A body has been found at a construction site across the city. He texts back that he'll be there as soon as he can. It's almost the end of class.

As the last student leaves, he grabs his keys and heads to his car. His equipment is always ready in the trunk, just in case.

Solve It!

Why do you think David is wearing glasses in this picture?

a) to keep dust from flicking into his eyes

b) because he can't see very well

c) it is a sunny day

Answers on page 45

Name: David Marek

Job: Forensic Anthropologist

Education: Studied for a degree in biology, then studied to be a Master of Forensic Anthropology and a Doctor of Physical Anthropology

Other jobs: Teaches forensic anthropology at a university

Career:
David has worked as a consultant for the police department for six years.

Favorite school subjects: Biology and history.

Favorite part of his job: You never know what the day will bring.

Worst part of his job: Some of the sights and smells can upset your stomach!

Most interesting case: David helped identify a victim buried way back in around 1680! The odd way the body had been buried led David to believe he had been murdered and dumped. The injuries to his bones showed he had a hard life and a violent death. David discovered a servant had gone missing in the area in around 1670. It is likely the body was his!

SPECIALIST SKILLS

Forensic anthropology is a specialist job. That means that not many people have the skills that David has learned. It takes years of training to become a forensic anthropologist. "Forensic" means to do with the law. Anthropology is the study of humans. A forensic anthropologist is a scientist who helps the police to identify human remains, often just from their bones.

Part-time Job?

Because cases where only bones are found are rare, forensic anthropologists often only work part-time solving crime. Like David, many also work teaching forensic anthropology at universities and colleges. It's great for the students to have a working forensic anthropologist teaching them. They know that their teacher's skills must be completely up-to-date!

Forensic anthropologists don't always go to the crime scene. Sometimes people at the scene will send David photographs of bones that have been found. This saves time, as often the bones are not human at all! Sometimes the bones are sent to the forensic anthropologist in a package, if the bones look as if they are from a burial rather than a crime scene. For this case, the Crime Scene Investigation team wants David to come and check the site. He can help decide what is just dirt, and what is important evidence.

EVIDENCE BAG CHALLENGE

Imagine you are a Crime Scene Investigator working at each of the crime scenes below. Should you send David a:

1 A dog brought its owner a bone it dug up from a grave at the old cemetery.

Photograph, package, or cab to collect him?

2 A man found some large bones in a dumpster behind the butcher's store.

Photograph, package, or cab to collect him?

3 A man finds a skull by a canal where a missing woman was last seen a year ago.

Photograph, package, or cab to collect him?

Answers on page 45

SCIENCE DETECTIVE

Know Your Bones

Forensic scientists need to be able to recognize every bone and know where it belongs on the skeleton. Do you know the names of any bones? Try this quiz and see if you know what part of the body these bones are from.

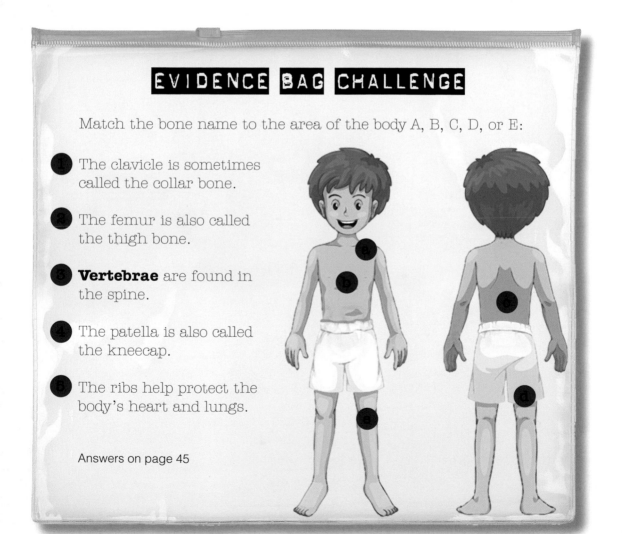

EVIDENCE BAG CHALLENGE

Match the bone name to the area of the body A, B, C, D, or E:

1. The clavicle is sometimes called the collar bone.

2. The femur is also called the thigh bone.

3. **Vertebrae** are found in the spine.

4. The patella is also called the kneecap.

5. The ribs help protect the body's heart and lungs.

Answers on page 45

Test your forensic anthropology skills. Can you match these skeleton parts to where they are found on the skeleton below? The answers are on page 45.

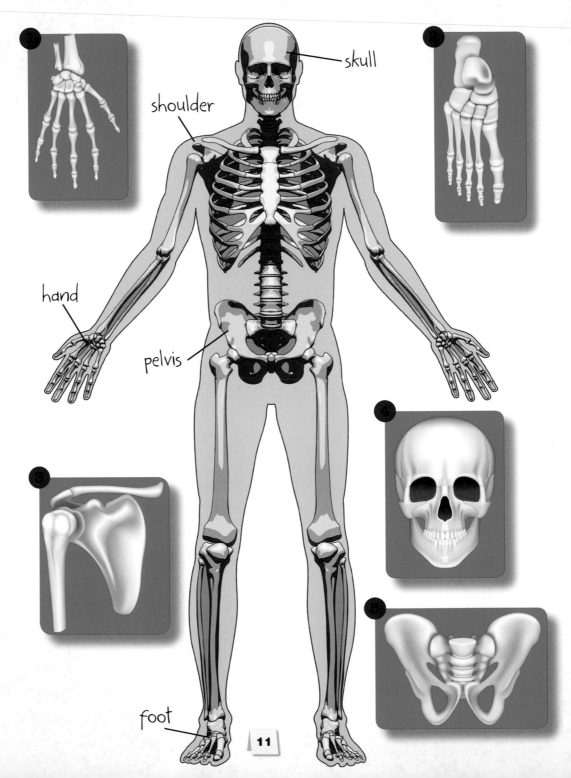

skull

shoulder

hand

pelvis

foot

Working as a Team

David arrives at the construction site. He is met by the detective in charge and the Crime Scene Investigation (or CSI) team. They ask David to check over the search area while the team carefully examines the site. They want to make sure they spot any pieces of bone among the dirt.

CSI has also asked for a forensic archaeologist to come to the crime scene. Forensic archaeologists are specially trained to search a crime scene, not just for bones, but also for evidence. The team all works together to try to find out who the victim is, what happened to them, and who's responsible. David's job is to focus on the bones.

Anthropology is the science of human beings.

Archaeology is the science of objects, buildings, and tools left by ancient peoples.

Solve It!

The CSI team spots a wedding ring poking out of the ground near the skeleton. Who's job is it to carefully dig out the ring?

a) the forensic anthropologist

b) the forensic archaeologist

Answers on page 45

Name: Paul Udoji

Job: Forensic archaeologist

Education: Studied for a degree in archaeology. Then studied for a master's degree in forensic archaeological science.

Other jobs: Is a college lecturer in forensic archaeology.

Career:
Paul first worked as an archaeologist. He took an interest in the crime-solving side of the work and went on to do his master's degree.

Favorite school subject: History.

Favorite part of his job: When all the hard work pays off and you find that important piece of evidence you were looking for.

Worst part of his job: Paul hates spending hours writing reports about what he has found.

Most interesting case: A skull found at the bottom of a hill made Paul suspicious that the body may first have been dumped elsewhere. He carefully searched the top of the hill and found some half-buried bones and the murder weapon.

Personnel File

Finding Buried Evidence

The team at the crime scene is experienced at looking for clues to where evidence may be. Even if something has been buried for a long time, there are still telltale signs above ground that help the experts.

Hunt the Evidence

Forensic archaeologist Paul scans the site. He is looking for any differences in the nearby soil.

- Is the soil lower or higher in one area?
  Soil removed to dig a grave is often left in a mound beside a burial site.

- Are there different plants growing in one area and not any other?
  Some plants prefer freshly dug, looser soil and will grow stronger there.

- Does any area of soil look darker than the surrounding earth?
  Disturbed soil tends to look darker in color.

All these signs may mean the soil underneath has been disturbed.

Top Tip

You can often tell if soil has been freshly dug if it feels loose when you push a **trowel** into it.

Soil

EVIDENCE BAG CHALLENGE

You will need: a trowel, an area of earth that it is OK to dig in, an old, small plastic toy, a pebble, a friend to challenge

Don't forget to check that the area you are digging in is OK to use, and the toy is OK to bury — and possibly lose!

Make sure your friend can't see what you are doing. Choose an area of soil to bury your toy. Dig a hole deep enough to cover the toy completely.

You need to remember where the toy is, so secretly mark the spot with a pebble. Don't make it look too obvious!

Challenge your friend to try to find the toy. Then swap over and let your friend bury the toy for you to find. Find a fresh area, so that the surrounding soil looks undisturbed.

Solve It!

You spot this change in soil at the crime scene. Which area should you start to dig in?

a) the area at the top of the photo

b) the area at the bottom of the photo

Answers on page 45

Skull's Secrets

It is warm in the spring sunshine. David kneels down and starts brushing some of the dirt away from the skull. The detectives search their computer database and find a list of people reported missing in the area over the years. It would be good for David to be able to tell them something about this skeleton as soon as possible.

A skull can tell a forensic anthropologist information about the victim. Sometimes it can give them a good idea whether the person was male or female.

Top Tip

David doesn't always need special tools. He uses a standard paintbrush to gently brush away dirt.

There are several ways to tell if a skull is male or female. Not all skulls will have all these differences, but if a skull has two or three, then an anthropologist can be pretty sure they've got it right.

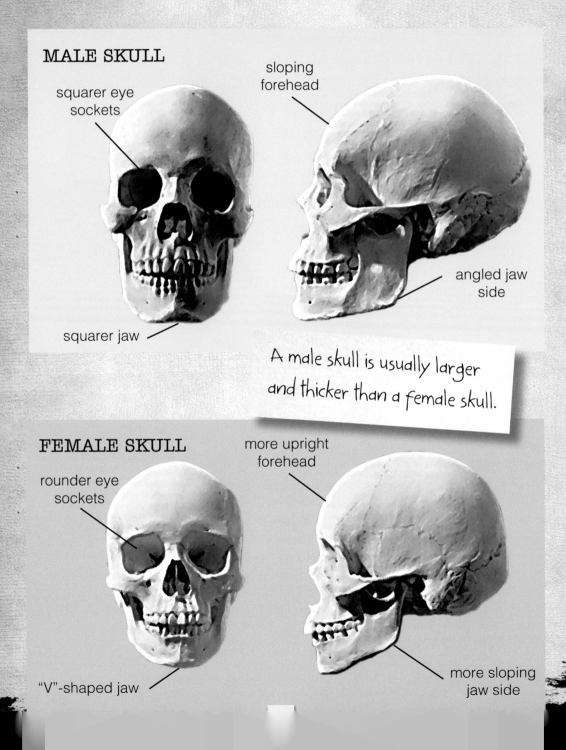

MALE SKULL

squarer eye sockets

sloping forehead

angled jaw side

squarer jaw

A male skull is usually larger and thicker than a female skull.

FEMALE SKULL

rounder eye sockets

more upright forehead

"V"-shaped jaw

more sloping jaw side

TELLTALE TEETH

Once David has cleared all the dirt away, he takes a look at the skull. He quickly works out if the skull is male or female and lets the detectives know. Then he starts to examine the teeth. There is a surprising amount of information you can find out from a skull's teeth.

If a skull is from a child, it is usually quite easy to tell the age from the teeth. Different types of teeth appear at particular ages. Adult skulls don't give away their age quite so easily.

Solve It!

The skull is quite small and lightweight. It has rounded eye sockets and a "V"-shaped jaw. David has told the detective what sex he believes the skull to be. Can you work it out from this description and the information on page 17?

a) a male

b) a female

Answers on page 45

18

All is not lost if the skull is from an adult though. Many people are identified from **dental records**. Police sometimes keep missing people's dental records on file. If they search the files and don't find a match, the style of dental work can tell a lot about the dentist. Police can sometimes tell when and where the dentist trained. Teeth can also reveal habits, such as if the victim bit their nails, or smoked. Sometimes David can tell if the victim played an instrument, or ate certain food.

Try Forensic Dentistry

If a case is tricky, David may call a forensic odontologist to help him. Forensic odontologists are tooth experts that help police identify victims just from their teeth.

The skull from the crime scene had a **fracture** on the lower jaw. The skull also had some work done on one of the front teeth. Can you decide which dental record belongs to our victim?

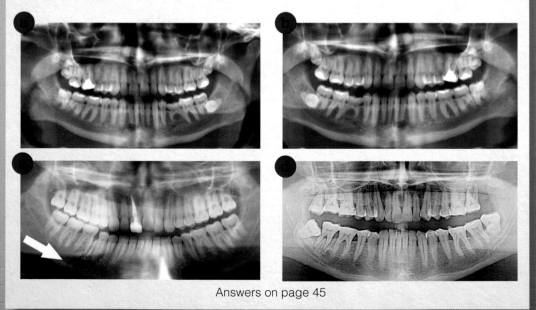

Answers on page 45

ny more bones?

The team searches the area close by. They don't find any other bones. David wonders how just a skull got to be buried next to a highway in Saunderstone. Is this skull from a crime scene at all? Once, David was called to a crime scene that was really just a prank. Some medical students had thought it was funny to leave a skull near a footpath on Halloween. Was there really a body buried here, or not?

David looks around the area to see if there are any clues. Could the construction work have damaged or moved the rest of the skeleton? Could the body have been placed somewhere nearby and the skull rolled down into this area from the nearby hill?

hill

stream

skull found here

woods

EVIDENCE BAG CHALLENGE

Try to construct the crime scene out of modeling clay and see if you can predict where your "skull" will roll.

You will need: modeling clay, cardstock

● Put your sheet of card on a table. Start to build your hills and valley out of modeling clay onto the cardstock.

● Try placing a small ball of clay at the top of a hill. Does it roll down? The hills don't need to be very sloped for the marble to begin to roll.

● Can you **predict** where the "skull" will end up? Try remodeling your hill to see if you can change its direction. Imagine that you are David. Would you be able to predict where the rest of the body was buried by where the skull ended up?

Solve It!

Where do you think the forensic team should start digging to find more bones?

a) at the top of the hill

b) along the stream

c) in the woods

d) a, b, and c

Answers on page 45

Scattered Skeleton

The team eventually finds a whole skeleton littered around the site. The team can get information about where the body was originally left by recording where each bone is found. What do you think the sketch below might tell them about where the body was buried? The answer is on page 45.

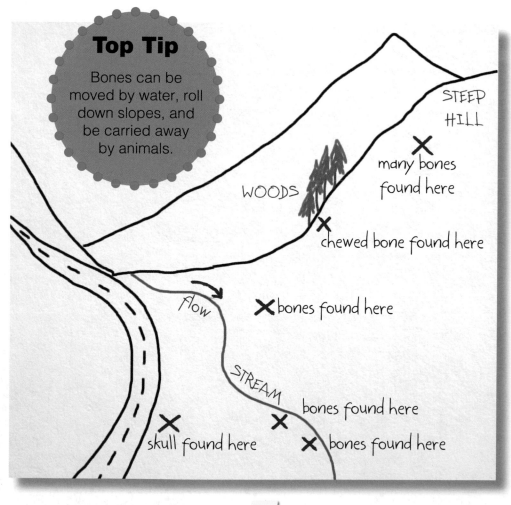

Top Tip

Bones can be moved by water, roll down slopes, and be carried away by animals.

STEEP HILL

X many bones found here

WOODS

X chewed bone found here

flow

X bones found here

STREAM

bones found here

X skull found here

X

X bones found here

Which Animal?

Which of these animals do you think might move buried bones?

a dog

b rabbit

c hamster

d snake

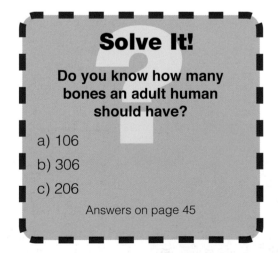

Answers on page 45

One way to tell if a skeleton is from a child or an adult is to count the number of bones. Because some of a child's bones haven't **fused**, or joined together, a child will have many more bones than an adult.

Solve It!

Do you know how many bones an adult human should have?

a) 106

b) 306

c) 206

Answers on page 45

ow most of the skeleton has been found, David is convinced that the body is of a female. The shape of the pelvis, the bone that forms the hips, looks female, and so does the skull. The bones show little sign of wear, so David believes the woman was between 21 and 40 years old. He wants to have the skull reexamined back at the lab. He can sometimes tell a person's **ancestry** from the shape of parts of their skull.

Before world travel became commonplace, people in different regions would develop slightly different shaped skulls over many generations. Forensic anthropologists can often tell if a skull's ancestry is either African, European, or Asian.

Top Tip

The teeth, jawbone, and the roof of the mouth can be most useful in telling the possible race of a skull.

Skull Differences

Can you match the descriptions to skulls A, B, and C and decide which is African, Asian, or European?

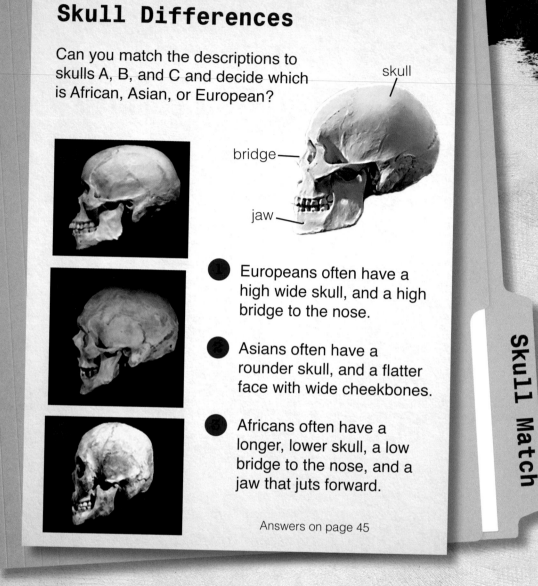

skull

bridge—

jaw—

1 Europeans often have a high wide skull, and a high bridge to the nose.

2 Asians often have a rounder skull, and a flatter face with wide cheekbones.

3 Africans often have a longer, lower skull, a low bridge to the nose, and a jaw that juts forward.

Answers on page 45

Answers on page 45

Skull Match

David takes the skull back to Ana at the lab, who examines it closely. She decides it definitely belongs to a female, who probably has European ancestry, but it was not certain. Often it is not obvious exactly what ancestry a person has. More and more people now have mixed ancestry. Also, some features such as skin color or eye shape can't be seen just from bones!

Can Bones Tell You Height?

Once a forensic anthropologist has an idea about the sex, ancestry, and age of a skeleton, they can try to work out the person's height. The leg bones are the most useful bone for telling a person's height.

David has to use different math to work out height depending on whether the bone was from a male or female. As people age they gradually get shorter, too, so a skeleton's age is important to estimate height. Even ancestry can alter what math David may use.

femur

Top Tip

As an estimate, the thigh bone, or femur, usually measures around a quarter of a person's height.

EVIDENCE BAG CHALLENGE

You will need: tape measure, some string, paper and pen

1. Test out whether a femur is really around a quarter of your height. Measure the length of your thigh bone from your knee to your hip.

2. Now measure your height. Write your measurements on some paper.

3. To work out whether your femur is a quarter the length of your height, multiply the femur length by four. Is the result your height?

4. Try measuring friends and family and see if anyone has a perfect 1:4 ratio of femur length to total body height. It often works better with adults.

Solve It!

Measure this small femur on the right. Can you work out about how tall the person it belonged to was?

a) around 2 foot 6 inches (80 cm)

b) around 5 foot 9 inches (180 cm)

c) around 3 foot 3 inches (100 cm)

Answers on page 45

earch for a cause of death

Sometimes David can get an idea how the person he is investigating may have died. Some injuries can be quite obvious, even to an untrained person. If the victim has a large hole in their skull, their death may have been caused by a gunshot wound or a heavy blow to the head.

Injuries

Ante, Peri, and Post

If a bone breaks before a victim dies, it is known as **antemortem**. If it breaks at the time of death, it is **perimortem**. A break that occurs after the victim is dead is called **postmortem**. Antemortem fractures will have signs of healing, while peri- and postmortem fractures will not. Perimortem breaks are usually clean, but postmortem breaks are usually messy.

David finds an antemortem break on one of the victim's leg bones. The victim had broken their leg at some point, and it had healed. This kind of information may help identify the victim from their medical records.

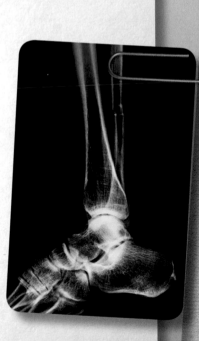

Solve It!

Are these injuries most likely to have have happened ante-, peri-, or postmortem?

a) a gunshot wound to the head

b) gnaw marks from an animal found on a leg bone

c) a healed, clean break to one of the bones in the arm

antemortem

perimortem

postmortem

Answers on page 45

Sometimes, when David is studying a victim's bones he finds evidence of **disease**. The disease may not be the cause of death, but it may help narrow down who the victim is by searching medical records of missing people. Illnesses such as bone cancer can be found by examining the **bone marrow**, the spongy tissue found inside bones. The body at Saunderstone had no obvious signs of any disease.

SCIENCE DETECTIVE

You Are What You Eat!

A skeleton can reveal where a person was born or raised. The food that we eat can affect our bones. By testing a **chemical** found in our bones known as carbon, forensic anthropologists can see whether a person had eaten a mainly wheat or corn-based diet.

A few hundred years ago, Europeans would mainly have eaten a wheat-based diet. Americans would have eaten a corn-based diet. If a skeleton found in America had mainly eaten wheat, anthropologists could be fairly sure they had only recently arrived in the country from Europe.

EVIDENCE BAG CHALLENGE

Could you guess who someone is from a list of the food they last ate? Try this challenge!

You will need: a few people who all know each other well, such as friends or family, a pen and some pieces of paper

1. Ask each person to write down everything they ate during the last four or five hours. It's best to do this late in the day.

2. Once the lists are finished, look at them and see if you can guess who wrote them.

3. Even if you can't narrow it down to one person, you may get some great clues. If two people ate the same thing, perhaps they are brother and sister? Or go to the same school?

Top Tip

If you think you could guess a person's handwriting, get your subjects to write each other's lists.

Sometimes it is possible to still see a body's stomach contents even if they have been dead for thousands of years! Some conditions, such as cold, icy places, can preserve a body. In Austria, a perfectly preserved man, known as Ötzi, was found around 5,000 years after he died. Scientists could still tell exactly what he had eaten in the hours before his death!

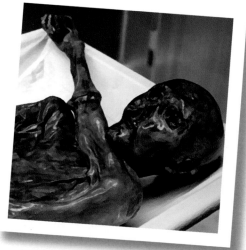

Ötzi

D etectives trying to discover who the victim was ask David to organize a **facial reconstruction**. David works with a **sculptor** to try to create a likeness of the victim using clues found on the skull.

David tells the sculptor any information he has found out about the person. She needs to know the ancestry, sex, and age of the victim. These facts all affect the thickness of clay she needs to use on different areas of the skull. Then the sculptor gets to work.

Top Tip

It is impossible to tell what color and style a victim's hair would have been. It is best to create a fairly standard hairstyle, like the one below.

A plaster cast is made of the skull. Pegs are put into the cast which mark the correct height the skin should come to around the skull. The sculptor then adds the clay to the height of the pegs. The sculptor uses any information David may have found out about the victim. If the victim had a broken nose, or jaw, for example, it may change the shape of the nose or chin. Other evidence the forensic archaeologists may have found nearby, such as jewelry, glasses, or hair ornaments, can also be useful in creating a likeness of the person.

EVIDENCE BAG CHALLENGE

You will need: modeling clay, knitting needle or skewer

1. Try to create your own clay model face. Think of someone you know that has an easy-to-recognize face. Perhaps they have a beard or wear glasses, or have no hair?

2. Take a large lump of clay and form the head and neck. Make the neck thick enough to support the head when you stand it up on a table.

3. Add the nose and ears, and any features such as hair or glasses. You can now add detail using the skewer or knitting needle. Draw in the eyes, eyebrows, and strands of hair.

4. Test out your likeness on some friends. See if anyone can recognize who it is!

Can You Identify the Victim?

The investigating team has pieced together some useful information about the victim. They have looked at local missing person files and found several that might belong to the skeleton. Look at the information below and then the information about each missing person. Can you decide which person is most likely to be our victim?

Victim File

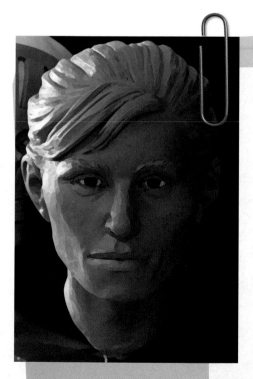

What Do We Know?

Sex: Female
Age: Adult, between 21–40
Ancestry: Probably European
Teeth: Root canal work on one front tooth
Broken bones: antemortem small fracture to lower jaw and lower leg bone break
Diseases: none obvious
Other information: may be married as a wedding ring was found at the site

MISSING: Annie Suter

Aged 25. Unmarried. Has Portugese and Indian ancestry. Knocked out a tooth in a riding accident in 2012. Suffering from bone cancer.

MISSING: Margot Schultz

Aged 59. Married. Has German ancestry. She had a broken leg in 1999. Dental records show work on one tooth and a minor jaw fracture.

Solve It!

Who's the victim?

a) Annie Suter
b) Margot Schultz
c) Sonia Smith
d) Georgie Pakeris

Answers on page 45

MISSING: Sonia Smith

Aged 32. Married. Has Ghanaian ancestry. She broke her leg in 2006. She had a fall while running, knocking out a tooth and hurting her jaw.

MISSING: Georgie Pakeris

Aged 28. Married. Has Lithuanian and Irish ancestry. She had a recent car accident, knocking out a tooth, fracturing her jaw, and breaking a leg.

Vital Clue

Back at the highway, Paul is searching the site for any clues to who the victim might be. He slowly examines the areas where bones were found. It is a large site, and it would be very easy to miss something.

He decides to use Ground Penetrating **Radar** (GPR) to help his search. GPR uses radar pulses, which reflect signals from objects under the surface of the soil. GPR is very good at finding metal objects. The equipment sometimes finds jewelry or even murder weapons.

Top Tip

An onboard computer records the strength and time taken for signals to reflect back. Operators can then look and see if the results are worth investigating.

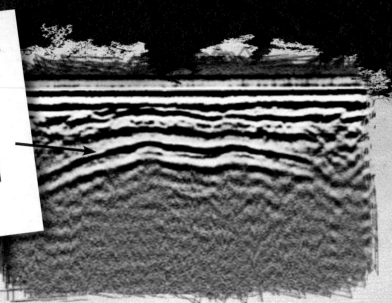

GPR can find burial sites as well as metal objects. This GPR image shows the arched roof of a large, underground burial chamber.

After several hours, Paul finds a vital piece of evidence. In mud near the crime scene, at the top of the hill, he finds an old vehicle license plate. Could this help identify the victim, or even better, lead to their killer? Detectives set to work tracing the numbers on the plate.

Recording Evidence

Whenever the team finds any evidence, they must record exactly where it was found. This information might be very important. Where an object was found may help solve the crime.

One of the best ways to plot where items have been found is to make a grid. Archaeologists divide up the site into squares using stakes and string. Usually the squares measure around 1 yard by 1 yard (1 m × 1 m). The team can then draw the grid onto a sheet of paper. They then mark where each object was found. Details about the time, the place, and the condition of the discovery are also written down.

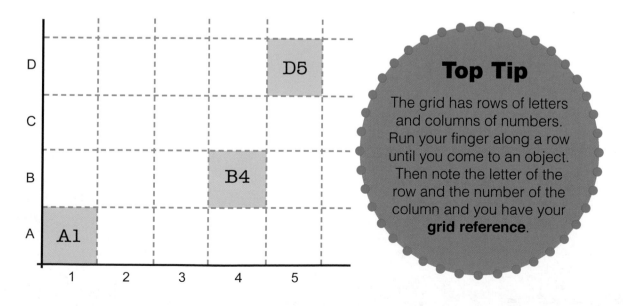

Top Tip

The grid has rows of letters and columns of numbers. Run your finger along a row until you come to an object. Then note the letter of the row and the number of the column and you have your **grid reference**.

Report Your Finds

Imagine you are helping David and Paul prepare their evidence. Can you match the grid references below to the correct object?

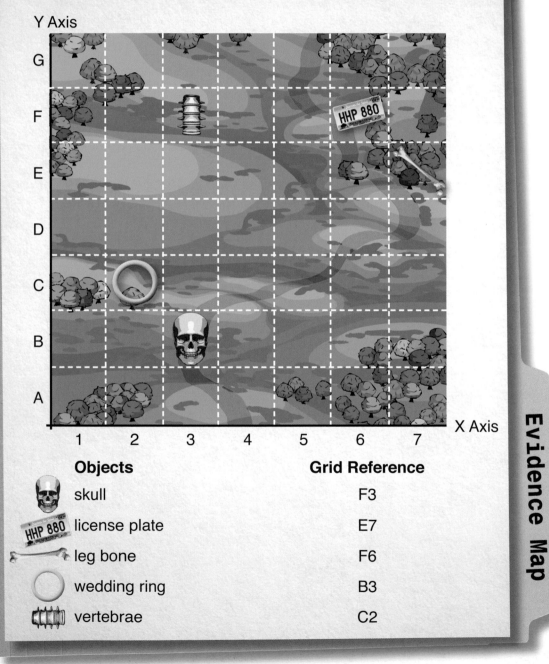

Objects		Grid Reference
	skull	F3
	license plate	E7
	leg bone	F6
	wedding ring	B3
	vertebrae	C2

The detectives on the case find the vehicle that matches the license plate found at the scene. This means they have traced who owned the vehicle around the time the body was dumped. They are also now sure the victim was Georgie Pakeris. The detectives are beginning to close in on the killer. David must look at his notes and prepare the evidence he will need to give in court.

The Report

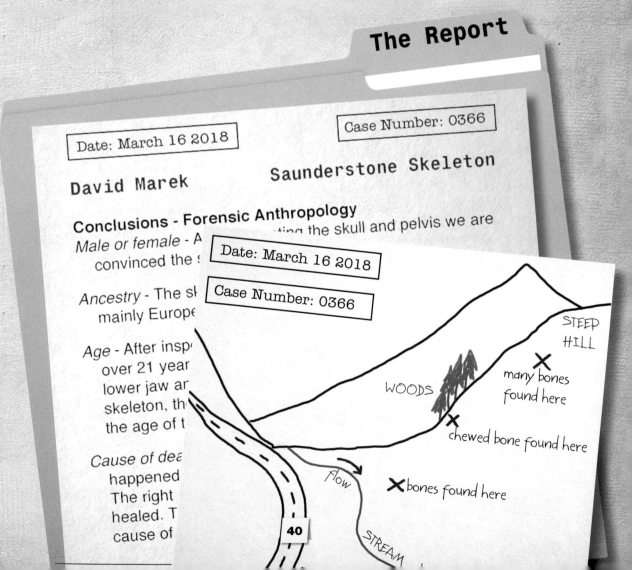

Date: March 16 2018

Case Number: 0366

David Marek

Saunderstone Skeleton

Conclusions - Forensic Anthropology

Male or female - A ...ting the skull and pelvis we are convinced the s...

Ancestry - The sk... mainly Europe...

Age - After insp... over 21 year... lower jaw ar... skeleton, th... the age of t...

Cause of dea... happened... The right... healed. T... cause of...

Date: March 16 2018

Case Number: 0366

STEEP HILL

WOODS

X many bones found here

X chewed bone found here

flow

X bones found here

STREAM

Witnesses in court need to be certain of their evidence. The lawyer **defending** the person accused of the crime will try their hardest to make sure their client does not go to jail. They will want to pick holes in everything you say. Could you rise to the challenge?

You will need: a friend, paper and pencil

● Look at the crime scene in the picture above. Write down any notes so you can remember the scene exactly. Make a quick sketch of the scene to help you remember.

● Now hand this book to your friend. Ask them to ask you questions about the crime scene. Be careful. If you give any wrong answers, the murderer will go free!

The Verdict

Tracing the license plate led detectives to an apartment block on the north side of Saunderstone. The plate belonged to a white pickup truck owned by John and Lorna Hadfield. The victim lived in the same apartment block as the Hadfields. Now they had a link between the victim and the suspects. It was time to take the Hadfields in for questioning. It wasn't long before John Hadfield confessed to the crime. But did he really do it?

Solve It!

John and Lorna Hadfield lived in the apartment below Georgie Pakeris and her husband, Lukas. John Hadfield was unwell and was in a wheelchair. Since the Pakerises moved in, John had hardly slept. His new neighbors were noisy. Other people in the apartment often heard the two couples shouting at each other. Some heard the Hadfields threaten to "shut Georgie up for good." What do you think happened the night Georgie Pakeris died? The jury will have to decide.

a) Lorna Hadfield got very angry late one night when she heard Lukas slam the door as he left. Lorna knocked on the Pakerises' door. When Georgie opened it, Lorna placed a bag over Georgie's head and tied it tight. She put Georgie in the back of her truck, hoping to frighten her. At the outskirts of Saunderstone, Lorna was going to let Georgie out to find her own way home. But to her horror, Georgie had suffocated! Panicked, Lorna drove the truck off-road, dragged Georgie out of the back, and buried her. John confessed to the crime to save his wife from prison.

b) A loud party from the Pakerises' apartment woke up John Hadfield. He was very angry. He grabbed a stone and wheeled himself to the elevator. When Georgie opened the door, he hit her with the stone. He then drove her body to the edge of Saunderstone and dumped her by the roadside.

Answers on page 45

Name: John Hadfield

Date of Trial: 12/14/2018
Court No: Court Two

Judge Presiding: R Marquez

Crime: Murder

Profile: John Hadfield had been arrested in 2015 for threatening people in the street. He was known to have a short temper. But he had been unwell for three years, and could no longer walk. He found driving difficult.

David is called to court as an expert witness. He looks through his notes and sketches the night before to remind him of all the facts. He is asked to describe what he found out about the skeleton. John Hadfield had confessed to the crime, but his story did not match David's evidence. There was no obvious damage to the skull of the victim. And how could John have moved the body? Why would John confess if it wasn't him? Now it's up to the jury to decide. What do you think?

GUILTY or **NOT GUILTY**

Glossary

ancestry From whom an individual, group, or species has come from.

antemortem Something that occurs before death.

bone marrow The soft, fatty, tissue that fills most bone cavities.

chemical A substance such as an element or compound.

crime scene The place where an offense has been committed and forensic evidence may be gathered.

defending Opposing the claim of another in a lawsuit.

dental records Records a dentist keeps about a patient's teeth.

disease Illness.

dispatched To send away quickly to a particular place or for a particular purpose.

evidence Material presented to a court in a crime case.

facial reconstruction The process of recreating the face of an individual whose identity is often not known from their skeletal remains.

fracture An injury resulting from the breaking of a bone.

fused Bones that joined together as they grew.

grid reference A map of a location using a series of vertical and horizontal grid lines identified by numbers or letters.

medical examiner An official who examines bodies of victims who experienced violent, sudden, or suspicious deaths.

perimortem Something that occurs at or near the time of death.

postmortem Something that occurs after death.

predict To decide in advance what will happen based on observation, experience, or reasoning.

radar A device that sends out radio waves for detecting and locating an object by the reflection of the radio waves and that may use this reflection to find out the position and speed of the object.

sculptor A person who makes sculptures, by carving, cutting, modeling, or casting melted metals into works of art.

trowel A small hand tool with a curved blade used by gardeners.

vertebrae The bones or cartilage that make up the spinal column, or backbone.

ANSWERS

page 5 - a, page 6 - a, page 9 - 1 = package, 2 = photograph, 3 = cab, page 10 - 1 = a, 2 = d, 3 = c, 4 = e, 5 = b, page 11 - 1 = hand, 2 = foot, 3 = shoulder, 4 = skull, 5 = pelvis, page 12 - b, page 15 - a, page 18 - b, page 19 - c, page 21 - d, page 22 - the body was probably left at the top of the hill, page 23 top - a, page 23 bottom - c, page 25 - a = 3, b = 1, c = 2, page 27 - a, page 29 - a = 2, b = 3, c = 1, page 35 - d, page 39 - skull = B3, license plate = F6, leg bone = E7, wedding ring = C2, vertebrae = F3, page 42 - a (John Hadfield confessed to protect his wife)

Want to be a
Forensic Anthropologist?

Job: Forensic anthropologist

Job Description: Forensic anthropologists work with law enforcement agencies and help examine skeletons. They study bones and gather information used to find out the individual's age at death, sex, and physical condition. They are often called on to testify in court as expert witnesses. The job is usually part-time. It may include night or weekend work. Forensic anthropologists may see some disturbing crime scenes, such as burials following war crimes or large-scale disasters such as plane crashes.

Qualifications needed: A degree in a science subject, then a further master's degree in forensic anthropology and then study to be a Doctor of Physical Anthropology. Experience working with the police force and with using lab equipment are essential. Photography skills and knowledge of how to use and read X-rays are useful.

Employment: Forensic anthropologists can work for police forces, museums, and the FBI. They often also teach forensic anthroplogy at universities.

Further Information
Books

Bedell, J. M. *So, You Want to Work with the Ancient and Recent Dead?: Unearthing Careers from Paleontology to Forensic Science.* New York, NY: Aladdin/Beyond Words, 2015.

MacLeod, Elizabeth. *Bones Never Lie: How Forensics Helps Solve History's Mysteries.* Toronto, Canada: Annick Press, 2013.

Websites

Reconstruct a skull at this interactive website!
http://kidsahead.com/external/activity/70

Take a virtual tour of a real forensic biology laboratory!
http://www.adfs.alabama.gov/VirtualTour.aspx

PUBLISHER'S NOTE TO EDUCATORS AND PARENTS:

Our editors have carefully reviewed these websites to ensure that they are suitable for students. Many websites change frequently, however, and we cannot guarantee that a site's future contents will continue to meet our high standards of quality and educational value. Be advised that students should be closely supervised whenever they access the Internet.